Holy Crocodile!

Stories of Saints and the Animals Who Helped Them

Caroline Cory

Our Sunday Visitor Publishing Division
Our Sunday Visitor, Inc.
Huntington, Indiana 46750

This book is dedicated to all the pets who have
inspired me over the years ...
especially my wire fox terriers, mutts, and pekes.

Our Sunday Visitor Publishing Division
Our Sunday Visitor, Inc.
200 Noll Plaza
Huntington, IN 46750

1-800-348-2440
bookpermissions@osv.com

ISBN: 978-1-61278-618-6 (Inventory No. T1314)
eISBN: 978-1-61278-309-3
LCCN: 2012953941

Cover and interior design: Rebecca J. Heaston
Cover and interior art: Caroline Cory

PRINTED IN THE UNITED STATES OF AMERICA
Graphics TwoFortyFour Inc., Wheaton, IL USA LT65080
January 2013

Introduction

The stories in *Holy Crocodile!* are based on actual legends of saints. These legends come from the Roman Catholic, Coptic, and Orthodox traditions and have been passed down since ancient times to inspire us.

Many tales tell of saints who help animals, but that's not the theme of this book. The stories here all have a unique twist: it's the animal, sea creature, insect, bird, or reptile who helps the saint.

The creatures in these stories come to the saint's aid because they recognize that person's goodness. A few saints offer help first, and are helped in return, but in most of these stories the saints are aided in answer to prayer. In almost all cases, the creatures act outside their instincts, or above and beyond their natural inclinations, to aid the saints.

These were special animals helping special people. When it comes to modern-day crocodiles, lions, snakes, and spiders — don't expect miracles! But feel free to train your dog or cat to help — so that they can be saintly too.

Pachome's Wild Ride

Pachome (Pa-KOHM) was hot and tired. He had walked a long way across the Egyptian desert before coming to a wide river. Needing to cross, he looked right and left. There was no bridge or boat in sight. Instead there were crocodiles. Crocodiles with large, bright, snapping teeth! Swimming the river was not an option. He prayed, "O God, show me a way across the river!"

As Pachome finished praying, a huge crocodile waddled up the riverbank toward him.

Pachome jumped back in fright, but the crocodile made no attempt to eat him.

Instead, the croc flashed his best toothy grin and wagged his tail back and forth.

Tossing his fearsome head, he indicated the opposite shore and nodded to Pachome to climb onto his back. Nervously, Pachome threw one leg over the back of the scaly beast. As soon as he sat down, the crocodile plunged into the water and swam speedily to the shore on the other side of the river.

Pachome got off and thanked the crocodile, and God, for bringing him safely across the river. The crocodile nodded as if to say, "You're welcome." From then on, whenever Pachome needed to cross the river, the crocodile would come and ferry him across.

Outfoxed

The fox was thrilled to find a rabbit in a trap, because rabbits are very tasty. He had just about finished eating it when the woodsman who had set the trap came along. The woodsman was so angry, when he saw the fox eating the rabbit he had wanted for dinner, he killed the fox. He didn't know that the fox was the king of Leinster's pet.

When the king heard that a man had killed his fox, he exploded with rage. He loved that fox and had taught it many tricks. The king had the woodsman arrested and announced he would chop off the man's head as punishment.

The woodsman's family begged the king to spare his life, but he refused. So the woodsman's wife and children raced from the palace straight to Brigid's home. Brigid was a wise, holy woman. They begged her to convince the king to spare the woodsman's life, because if anyone could get the king to show mercy, it would be Brigid.

Brigid set off for the castle, taking a shortcut through the woods. As she walked, a fox trotted up beside her. "You're a pretty fox," she said. "I wonder if you are smart." She held out her hand for the fox to sniff, and since it seemed tame, she began to teach it tricks. "Sit. Roll over. Play dead." The fox learned quickly, much to Brigid's delight.

When Brigid got to the castle, she marched right in to see the king. The fox followed behind her. "Please, sire," she said, "spare the life of the woodsman. He's very sorry and will never kill a fox again."

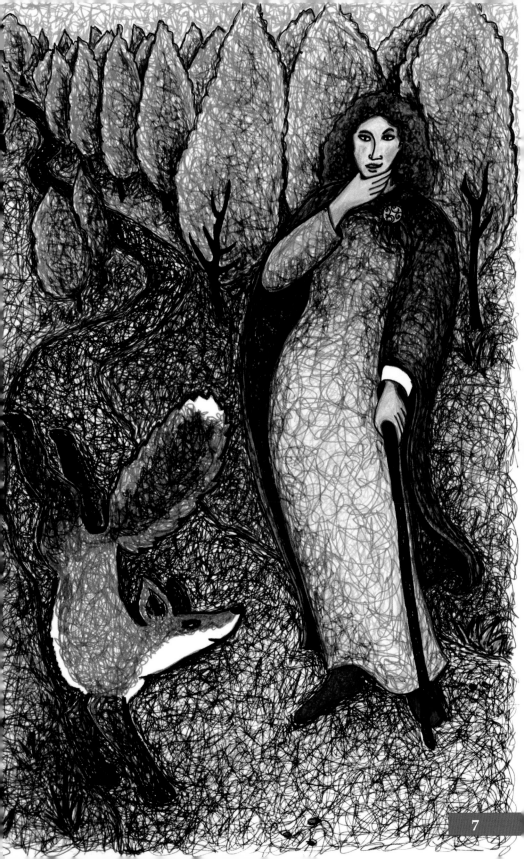

"That fox wasn't just any fox!" the king cried out. "I loved him. I taught him tricks. It's only fair that since the woodsman killed my fox, the woodsman must die!"

Brigid answered, "Fair? But if you kill the woodsman, you will hurt his whole family. They might starve, and that's not fair. Besides, Jesus tells us to forgive." The king was so angry, he did not want to hear about fairness or forgiveness.

So Brigid wisely changed the subject. "I understand how special a pet fox is. I have one who can do tricks too, and I would feel terrible if someone killed him."

All this time the fox had been hiding behind Brigid's skirt, and the king had not seen it. Now Brigid made a clicking noise, and the fox circled in front of her and sat down. The king's eyes grew teary: the beautiful animal looked like a twin of his dead pet. Brigid asked her fox to sit, beg, roll over, and jump. The king clapped his hands when he saw all the tricks this fox could do.

Brigid knelt and whispered to the fox, who seemed to nod in agreement. Then she stood up and offered the king a deal. "I will give you my fox," she said, "in exchange for the woodsman's life and freedom." The king was so charmed by her fox that he agreed. The woodsman was freed.

So the fox went to live in the palace. Perhaps it grew bored with royal life. Perhaps it never really liked the king. Or perhaps it felt the debt was paid. At any rate, after a few years, Brigid's fox ran away, back to the wild.

Medard's Umbrella

Medard was absentminded. He would marvel at God's creation and trip over a log because he wasn't watching where he was going. He would be praying and grab the wrong coat. He would thank God for his dinner and forget to feed the dog, until the barking reminded him.

One afternoon Medard went for a walk. He was busy listing all his blessings and didn't notice it was about to rain. The sky turned gray, then purple and black as big storm clouds formed. A few raindrops splashed on the path in front of Medard, but he paid no attention as he was counting blessing number 364. Finally, rain began to pour. Everyone caught outside without an umbrella got soaking wet. Except Medard.

In the countryside, Medard said hello to some folks huddling under a tree to get out of the rain. Medard saw they were wet and thanked God he was dry (blessing 426). He didn't notice they were staring and pointing as he passed by.

In town, everyone was drenched. Medard continued to thank God, but he began to wonder why he was the only one who was dry. Everyone that Medard passed would stop, stare, and point over his head.

Finally, Medard noticed and tilted his head back to see what everyone was pointing at. An eagle hovered over his head. It had begun flying over him when the rain started and had followed his every step. By spreading its wings wide, the eagle had kept him dry.

After that day, whenever it rained, the eagle flew over Medard to keep him dry. He never had to carry an umbrella again. Which was just as well, because he never remembered to take one anyway.

The Dog
Who Wouldn't Give Up

Roch (ROCK) and his little dog were walking to Rome on a pilgrimage. As they approached a village, a man called out, "Run away! The black plague is here!" The plague was a terrible disease! Most people who got it died. Roch could hear sick people crying for help. "A good Christian wouldn't walk away," he said to himself.

So Roch and his dog went door to door, nursing people who were sick and dying. After a few weeks, Roch noticed a black sore on his leg. He had caught the plague! Roch walked to the woods and laid himself down by a stream. He thought this was a good place to die, where he wouldn't burden anyone. His little dog followed him.

"Go back to the village," Roch ordered the dog. "If you stay with me, you will starve." The dog ignored him and sat down to watch over his friend. After Roch fell asleep, the dog began to get hungry. He didn't want to starve. Quietly he got up and crept away.

Roch woke to dog kisses. While he slept, the dog had gone begging for food. He brought Roch a loaf of bread, with only a nibble missing. Roch ate some and gave the rest to the dog.

Each day the dog begged in the village. People gladly gave him food because they knew he belonged to the man who had nursed their sick. Roch ate what his dog brought him and got stronger. He recovered from the plague because his dog refused to give up on him. When Roch was well, they continued on their way to Rome.

A Sweet Deal

Modomnoc (Moh-DOM-nock) was the beekeeper for an abbey in Wales. He was gentle with his bees. He sang to them and carried their hives to fields full of bright flowers with delicious nectar. His bees made the sweetest honey and purest beeswax.

Modomnoc liked beekeeping but felt it wasn't his calling. He wanted to study to become a priest in Ireland. So Modomnoc hired a boat to ferry him across the Irish Sea. He waved good-bye to his friends and set sail.

After going a short distance, Modomnoc heard a familiar buzzing sound. His bees were following the boat! "No, no!" he said to the bees. "Turn back! You're the abbey's bees, not mine. Go home!" The bees wouldn't listen and continued to follow the boat. Finally Modomnoc asked the sailors to turn around so that the bees would follow the boat back to Wales.

After landing, Modomnoc walked the bees back to their hives. He sternly commanded the bees to stay, then sailed away again. The boat was a bit farther across the sea when Modomnoc heard the bees swarming a second time. Again he asked the sailors to turn around so that he could return the bees. He walked the bees back to the abbey again. The abbot said to Modomnoc, "If the bees follow you a third time, take them to Ireland with my blessing."

Modomnoc set sail, and the bees followed him again. This time he called the bees to the boat and let them rest on the sails, while continuing on to Ireland. It turned out that Modomnoc's calling was to be a priest ... and the first beekeeper in Ireland.

A Staggering Adventure

Ciaran (KEAR-on) was generous and everyone knew it. People came to the monastery, where he lived, whenever they needed help. Ciaran always gave something: advice, a bit of bread, a helping hand, or a gold coin.

The other monks who lived with Ciaran were not so generous. They grumbled when he gave things away. One day Ciaran gave away the chicken meant for dinner. That night, the monks were very crabby, eating dry bread and turnips, instead of juicy chicken. They told Ciaran he had to stop giving things away ... or he had to leave.

Ciaran was sad to leave but knew it was for the best. He packed a bag and said good-bye. Outside, a stag stood by the monastery door. It seemed to be waiting for him, so Ciaran said, "I'll follow you. I think you know where I need to go better than I do." The stag nodded. Ciaran hoisted his pack on the stag's back and the two began to walk.

Ciaran followed the stag though the woods, over rivers and streams, around the edges of towns, down into valleys, and up over hills. He followed the stag for months, walking a very long way. At last, the stag led Ciaran across a sandy ocean beach, at low tide, to a place called Hare Island. In a beautiful field near the water, the stag shrugged off Ciaran's pack.

"Are we here?" Ciaran asked. The stag nodded yes.

Ciaran built a new monastery on the spot the stag chose for him. Men flocked to join his monastery. All of Ciaran's new monks were generous, and they never lacked good things to give to people in need.

Let's Make a Deal

Gall liked being a hermit: living alone, far away from other people. He built a home in the deep woods and lived there happily for many years.

But as he grew old, Gall felt lonely. It was also hard to do everything for himself. He wished he had a friend to help with chores and to keep him company.

One day Gall was making acorn bread. The baking bread filled the air with the smell of nuts and honey. A bear sniffed a whiff of it on the breeze. He turned in circles to discover which direction the delicious odor came from, and then took off with a trot.

In the meantime, Gall was getting cranky. His bread was only half-baked, and he was running out of firewood. "My old bones are too tired to gather more wood," he complained. Then Gall saw a bear step out of the woods, nose in air, sniffing his way toward the bread oven. The bear licked his lips; it was clear what he wanted: Gall's bread!

"Brother Bear," Gall said, "let's help each other. I'll share my freshly baked bread if you'll carry firewood for me."

Gall went into the woods and mimed picking up large branches. The bear understood and picked up a big log. Walking on his back legs, the bear followed Gall to his oven, where he dropped the wood. Gall added the log to the fire. When the bread finished baking, Gall gave the bear a loaf. It was the best thing the bear had ever tasted!

After that, the bear came every day with logs for the fire, ate quite a lot of bread, and became Gall's best friend.

Cuthbert's Chilly Night

One warm evening, Cuthbert went for a swim. He loved to swim in the sea. The cold water was refreshing. After paddling about a bit, Cuthbert stood in the water and watched the sunset. He saw sea otters playing in the distance and thanked God for all creatures and the beauty of creation. He continued to pray as the tide rose up to his chest.

When Cuthbert ended his prayers, the moon glowed brightly. He hadn't noticed how numb and cold he had become while praying. Goosebumps pricked his skin, and he was shivering down to his bones. The shore seemed a long way off. He tried to swim, but he could barely move. His arms and his legs felt like dead weights. "Oh, God! Help me!" he gasped.

As he struggled to keep his head above water, Cuthbert felt a hot tingle on his big toe. Then came a patch of heat along his back. Warm things bumped, jostled, and nudged Cuthbert under the water.

A furry head popped above the waves and looked Cuthbert in the eye. The friendly creature licked his cheek with a big, warm tongue. A sea otter! Otters surrounded Cuthbert, warming him up. One licked his feet, another his hands. A small otter tickled his elbow, while a huge otter kissed his ear.

Cuthbert felt warmth washing over him as the otters licked him back to life. Soon Cuthbert was able to swim to shore, guided by his otter friends.

Dancing Snakes

Abanoub (Ah-BAH-noob) was an Egyptian boy, when Egypt was under Roman rule. He was an orphan, so he didn't have to ask his parents' permission when he decided to travel around the country to tell people about Jesus.

Abanoub went to the marketplace in the city of Atrib. He began to tell the fish sellers about the miracle of Jesus multiplying the fishes. People were interested in Abanoub's stories and curious about his faith.

This worried the governor of the city. His boss, the Roman emperor, did not like Christianity. To please the emperor, the governor ordered his soldiers to put the boy into a pit filled with hundreds of poisonous snakes. By killing Abanoub, the governor hoped to scare people away from becoming Christian.

Abanoub's heart beat hard with fear as he was lowered into the pit, but he remembered to pray. The snakes hissed but did not strike. Abanoub sang to keep his courage up. The snakes swayed and danced to his songs.

A day later, Abanoub was still alive! No one could believe it. The soldiers pulled him out of the pit and brought him before the governor. In their hurry, they didn't notice a snake wrapped around Abanoub's waist like a belt.

At the palace, the snake quickly slithered away from Abanoub. It coiled itself around the governor's neck, preparing to strike him dead. The governor cried, "Be merciful, Abanoub! Pray to your God so that the snake doesn't hurt me!"

Abanoub knew that Jesus said, "Love your enemies," so he prayed. The snake uncoiled itself and went away, sparing the governor's life.

A Bird in the Hand

When Kevin was seven, he walked far into the woods. He knelt beneath a tree and closed his eyes. Cupping his hands together, he began to pray. He thanked God for his blessings, imagining the Holy Spirit, in the form of a dove, filling his hands with gifts.

After Kevin prayed awhile, his hands felt full. Had the Holy Spirit really put gifts in them? Curious, Kevin opened his eyes. Instead of a dove, a blackbird sat on his thumb. She had built a nest in his hands and laid her eggs there.

Kevin debated what to do. If he put the nest on the ground, the eggs might break or animals might eat them. On the other hand, he was ready to go home for lunch. "Little bird," Kevin said, "I'll help you, if you help me." As the blackbird watched, Kevin opened his mouth wide and stuck out his tongue. He had seen baby chicks do this when they wanted to be fed.

The blackbird nodded and flew off. She came back with a big juicy worm and dangled it over Kevin's mouth. He wasn't *that* hungry! He shut his mouth tightly and shook his head no. With a shrug, the bird swallowed the worm and flew off. She returned with berries. Kevin opened his mouth and let her feed him.

Kevin prayed for time to pass quickly. Soon the chicks hatched. The mother bird flew back and forth constantly, bringing worms, nuts, and berries to feed her brood and Kevin. When the chicks fluttered out of the nest, Kevin said good-bye to the blackbird and returned home. His worried family forbade him to ever go into the woods again.

Thrown to the Lions

It was against the law to be Christian in ancient Rome, but Prisca couldn't keep her faith a secret. By the time she was thirteen, she had told so many people she was Christian, no one was surprised when she was arrested.

Claudius, the emperor of Rome, said that any Christian who agreed to worship the Roman gods would be set free. Otherwise, they would be thrown to the lions!

Prisca knew in her heart she could never stop loving Jesus, so she refused to sacrifice to the old gods. Roman soldiers took her to the arena. Gladiators fought there, and wild animals tore apart Christians and ate them, to amuse the crowds.

Prisca was scared as she waited to go into the arena. She heard screaming and smelled blood. She started to sing a hymn to make her feel a little bit braver. The crowd booed when Prisca walked into the arena. Even though they liked blood sports, they were unhappy to see such a young girl become lion bait.

Two ferocious lions charged toward Prisca. Terrified, she closed her eyes and continued to sing in a shaky voice. Minutes passed, and Prisca wondered why she hadn't yet been eaten. She opened her eyes. The lions had stopped a few feet away from her. They seemed to be listening to her song. Coming closer, the big cats purred, and one gently licked her feet.

Prisca stroked the lion's great mane. She was no longer afraid. The lions were friends and wouldn't eat her. The crowd cheered in amazement. Prisca sang a song of joy as she petted the lions, who were now tame as kittens.

27

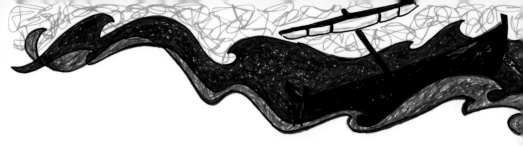

A Whale of a Surprise!

Brendan believed the Garden of Eden was on an island. So he bought a boat and convinced a crew to join him in looking for it.

Easter morning, months after they had set sail, Brendan said, "We need to find an island where we can celebrate Easter Mass." A sailor pointed to a bump rising out of the ocean. "There's a small, barren island that's just big enough."

They anchored at the island and went ashore. Suddenly, the earth rose and shifted. "Earthquake!" a man yelled. But the ground wasn't shaking; it was slowly rising out of the water. Then the island started to move, dragging the boat with it. The terrified men threw themselves to the ground and hugged it tightly.

Brendan was hanging over one side of the island, trying not to fall, when he saw an eye staring up at him. They weren't on an island. They were on the back of a whale! "Sister Whale," Brendan said, "I'm sorry we thought you were an island. We wanted to celebrate Easter Mass, and your broad back seemed like a good place." Looking at Brendan, the whale blinked as if she understood. "Since we're already here, would you let me say Mass?"

The whale stopped swimming. She blinked yes. Brendan stood up and announced to the crew, "We're having Mass with our friend, the whale."

Brendan and his men sailed the seas for seven years. They never found Eden. But every Easter the whale would find them, and they would celebrate Mass on her back.

The Tot and the Wolf

A ilbe (AISLE-bee) was old enough to walk and toddle happily after butterflies. One day, he followed a pretty yellow one deep into the woods. Ailbe didn't know it, but he was lost. As the day wore on, he became hungry, and the shadows in the forest started to frighten him. Ailbe sat and wailed. He did not know what else to do.

Ailbe was far from the village, so nobody heard him crying or came to his rescue. A wolf passing nearby wondered what all the noise was about. The wolf followed the cries until she found Ailbe.

The wolf sniffed Ailbe — she had never seen a human baby before. She wasn't sure what kind of creature Ailbe was, but she could tell he was young, unhappy, and hungry. Like any good mother, the wolf wanted to help. With her teeth, she gently picked Ailbe up by the back of his shirt and carried him to her den. She set Ailbe down among her cubs. Soon Ailbe was laughing with delight as his new wolf brothers and sisters jumped around him. The wolf mother treated Ailbe like one of her own: she fed him and kept him warm and safe.

One day a hunter saw Ailbe playing in the woods near the wolf den. He picked Ailbe up and carried him back to his village. At first, Ailbe cried for his wolf family, but soon he got used to living with people again.

When Ailbe grew older, he became a monk. The old wolf came to his monastery to beg for food. Ailbe recognized her, called her his mother, and fed the wolf food from his table.

The Cat
Who Played Fetch

Clare loved to listen to her friend Francis talk about God. She was so inspired that she felt as if her heart was on fire. Clare decided to give her life to God and become a nun.

Clare and the other nuns prayed, sang, and worked every day. When Clare grew older, she was often sick and had to stay in bed. She could no longer weed the garden, knead bread, dip candles, or sing with the choir. But even in bed, Clare could sew.

Clare stitched beautiful cloths for the altar. She made scarves for the nuns and hats for the poor. The nuns' cat purred by her side as she sewed. The cat made Clare laugh as she batted balls of yarn or swatted thread dangled in front of her.

Then one afternoon — bump! Clare's elbow knocked a roll of fabric off her narrow bed. Clare and the cat watched the cloth bounce and unroll across the room and out of reach. Clare sighed. She was too weak to get out of bed and pick it up.

The cat looked from Clare to the fabric and meowed. She jumped off the bed and began to nudge the cloth with her paws and nose. She turned the cloth over and over — all the way back to the bed!

When the fabric was close enough for Clare to reach it, the cat jumped back onto the bed. She looked at Clare, as if to say, "What a fun new game. Let's play it again sometime!"

After that, the cat would fetch whatever accidentally flipped off the bed, bounced off the table, or rolled across the floor.

The Web of Deception

Felix had been running so fast that his lungs hurt and knees wobbled. Emperor Decius had ordered the arrest of all Christians who wouldn't make sacrifices to the Roman gods. When soldiers came to arrest Felix, he ran. But now he couldn't run much farther.

Felix ducked inside an abandoned building. The light was dim, but he could see there were no good hiding places: just cracked walls tumbling down. Felix heard the shouts of the

soldiers drawing nearer. Trapped, with nowhere else to go, Felix wedged himself between a wide crack in the crumbling walls. It was a ridiculous place to hide, not deep enough or dark enough, but Felix couldn't run anymore.

Felix closed his eyes and prayed to God, "Please make me invisible!" That was the only way the soldiers were not going to see him. Felix held his breath. He heard the soldiers asking one another which way he had gone. He expected a soldier to pull him from his hiding place any moment, shouting, "Here he is!"

Instead, the soldiers' voices grew dimmer, and their footsteps faded away. Amazed that he hadn't been found, Felix opened his eyes. Everything looked gray and gauzy. He was confused.

Then Felix realized that hundreds of spiders had rapidly spun webs over the crack in the wall where he hid. The webs were layered so thickly that they looked as if they had been there for years. The soldiers had walked right by and never seen Felix. The spiderwebs had made him invisible, in answer to his prayers.

Every Little Bit Counts

Gudwall was looking for a new home when he found a cave next to the sea. He congratulated himself on finding such a delightful place to live. It was a hot summer, and the fresh sea breeze cooled the cave beautifully.

As the weather got colder, the wind blew briskly through the cave. Most people would have moved away, but Gudwall just wore warmer clothes and spent more time praying under his blankets.

One winter night, a terrible storm came up. The wind-whipped waves bashed against the rocks in front of Gudwall's home. The sea lapped over the mouth of the cave as the water rose higher.

Gudwall looked outside and saw he was trapped! The path leading from his cave to the rest of the island was under water. The sea was continuing to rise, and Gudwall realized that his cave would flood and he would drown.

Gudwall called on God for help. As he prayed, he saw fish of all sizes and shapes swim by his cave. Each swam up, paused, and turned around. Where the fish stopped, a brown patch appeared beneath the waves. That spot quickly turned into a sandy ridge.

Now Gudwall could see that each fish carried a pebble or a grain of sand in its mouth, which it spit out to make a breakwater. The fish were building a wall to keep the waves from flooding the cave. Each fish made many trips with sand or stones until the wall was big enough that the waves couldn't pass over it.

"Thank you, God, for little fishes!" Gudwall exclaimed, and he moved out of the cave the next day.

Raven to the Rescue

Benedict was an abbot in charge of a monastery full of quarrelsome monks and priests. When his job became too stressful, Benedict would relax by going camping.

One day, as Benedict was preparing to go away, a priest came by with freshly baked bread. "Please enjoy this loaf I baked for your journey," the priest said. Benedict took the bread with surprise. He thought this priest didn't like him. How nice to be wrong!

Arriving at his usual campsite, Benedict greeted a raven sitting on a rock. She and Benedict were old friends. The raven liked to sit on his shoulder and be fed crumbs of bread.

Benedict sat down and took the lovely, golden bread from his sack. The raven hopped on his shoulder. Benedict was about to break and share the bread when the raven squawked angrily. She grabbed the whole loaf in her claws and flew away.

Benedict yelled, "Come back!" — but the raven flew higher. Flying over a nearby river, she dropped the loaf. It tumbled through the air and into the water. "Greedy bird!" Benedict scolded. "Now neither of us will get to eat that tasty bread!"

Just then, a young monk came running up the hill, shouting, "Don't eat the bread!" He explained that the bread had been poisoned! The priest who had baked it wanted to kill Benedict so that he could become the abbot. But after Benedict left, the priest saw how evil his actions were, repented, and confessed.

Benedict thanked God for his friend the raven. She sensed the bread was deadly and saved his life.

The Squeaky Alarm Clock

Colman worried he wasn't a very good abbot. He and his monks had the best job in the world: to pray for God's love. They prayed before breakfast, lunch, dinner, and at bedtime. They also prayed twice in the middle of the night. Or, they meant to. But all of the monks — especially Colman — slept soundly.

As abbot, it was Colman's responsibility to wake everyone up. Instead, he almost always slept through night prayers. Sadly, alarm clocks hadn't been invented yet.

A mouse lived in a hole in Colman's bedroom wall. He had tamed it by feeding it crumbs of bread and cheese. One night Colman was feeding and petting his mouse while talking to himself. "Tonight I must, must, must, wake up! We can't miss night prayers again. I have to wake up at midnight!"

Colman said goodnight to his little friend and tucked himself into bed. Soon he was fast asleep. In a dream, a feather brushed across Colman's ear. He scratched the tickle but didn't wake up. He dreamed that little fairy feet danced across his forehead, but he still didn't wake up. Then he dreamt that an alligator was biting his toes! Colman woke up with a start. He saw his blanket had slipped off his feet — and his pet mouse was gnawing his big toe.

Colman looked at the candle with hour markings. It was exactly midnight. Time to wake the other monks! Rejoicing, Colman thanked the mouse for waking him. From then on, the mouse became Colman's alarm clock, waking him gently by nibbling his ears or tickling his nose … or on nights the abbot slept too soundly, biting sharply on his toes!

Hold Steady

Cainnic (CAIN-ick) loved books. Every day, he read his Bible and legends of saints. He owned books about science and art. Books lay on his table, on his shelves, on his bed, and on the floor. Some had colorful pictures, others just black ink. He had thick books copied by monks in faraway lands and slim volumes he had written himself.

Cainnic liked to sit outside, in the sunshine, to read. He lived a hermit's life, alone with no one to talk to, but he kept from being lonely by reading aloud to himself. He read in a deep voice for sad stories and a laughing voice for funny ones. One day, after reading a particularly fine passage of the Bible, Cainnic noticed a stag standing on the edge of the forest, who appeared to be listening.

The stag started waiting outside Cainnic's door for story time. Once, the hermit brought out a big book and began to read. Just as the story was getting interesting, he closed the book. "I'm sorry," he said to the stag. "I have to stop. This book is so heavy, I can't hold it up anymore."

When the stag heard this, he butted his head at the book as if to say, "Don't stop now!" He pushed the book so hard that it flipped into the air and snagged on his antlers. The stag pranced in front of Cainnic, pleased with himself.

Cainnic understood. He opened the book and wedged it between the stag's antlers, then found his place and began to read. The stag supported and shared Cainnic's love of books ever after.

The Misunderstood Lion

"ROAR! Whine ... whimper ... whimper...."

Gerasimos (Ju-RAY-zee-mos) heard the cry of pain and went to help. He found a lion sitting under a tree, crying and licking its paw. A sharp, thorny stick was stuck between the lion's toes. The lion growled, but the man remained calm. "I can help you," he said. So the lion let him pull out the thorn.

The lion was so grateful to Gerasimos that he decided to follow him home. Gerasimos lived in a monastery. The other monks were fearful, seeing a lion at their door. Gerasimos told them that the lion wanted to become part of their community and had nodded yes when Gerasimos asked him if he was willing to become a vegetarian.

The lion was given the job of guarding the monastery's donkey. The donkey's important job was to carry water to the monks who worked in the fields. Every day, the lion and the donkey delivered water. Over time, the two became friends, and they would stop along their route to eat berries or take naps.

One morning, on their way to the fields, the donkey found some sweet grass to eat. The lion wasn't interested in grass, so he curled up for a quick nap in the shade of some bushes. As the lion slept, a robber came down the trail. He saw the donkey and decided to steal him, since there was no owner in sight. The donkey tried to bray and wake up the lion, but the robber whisked him away too quickly.

When the lion woke up, the donkey
was nowhere to be seen. Ashamed that he
had lost the donkey, he went to find Gerasimos.
When Gerasimos saw the lion without the donkey, he
assumed the worst. He thought the lion had eaten the
donkey! The poor lion couldn't speak to defend himself.
Gerasimos punished the lion by giving him the donkey's job of
carrying the heavy water jars. Since the lion felt guilty about losing
his friend, he humbly took on the donkey's task.

Months later, the lion saw a man leading a donkey, roped
together with three camels, down the road. At the sight of the
monastery, the donkey stopped and refused to go any farther. The
man began to beat the donkey, who brayed in distress. When the
lion heard the donkey's cries, he recognized his old friend. Roaring,
he leaped to the rescue. When the robber saw a roaring lion
charging his way, he ran away as fast as he could. He left behind his
stolen camels and donkey, figuring the lion would eat them, instead
of him.

The donkey and the lion greeted each other happily. The lion picked up the rope in his mouth and led the donkey and the camels to Gerasimos. Seeing the donkey alive, Gerasimos realized he had misjudged the lion. The monks found the owners of the camels and returned them. The robber never returned for fear of the lion. And the lion and the donkey resumed their work and their friendship.

Gerasimos gave the lion the name Jordanes. Jordanes was a faithful member of the community for many years. When Gerasimos died, the lion stayed near the grave, mourning, until it was his turn to leave this world.

About the Author

Caroline Cory has always loved animals and saints. Her earliest memory is the thrill of meeting a little black dog when she was one year old. As a four-year-old, she loved picture stories from the Bible, particularly Daniel in the lions' den and Elijah being fed by ravens. She was fascinated with saints and martyrs: as a seven-year-old, she used to dress Barbie in a toga and throw her to the (stuffed toy) lions!

So compiling a book of animals and saints was a natural labor of love for Caroline.

Being a dog owner, Caroline was initially caught by the story of St. Roch's little dog — figuring that any dog willing to share its food is halfway to animal "sainthood." From there, she began a long (pre-Internet!) quest to find other stories of animals who had helped saints.

The drawings in this book were done primarily in ink, with color pencil providing skin tones. Caroline likes to scribble, and she hopes her scribbly style will inspire others to scribble more.